CRAFT IT!

Birthday

Gifts

Anastasia Suen

Rourke
Educational Media

rourkeeducationalmedia.com

TABLE OF CONTENTS

MATERIALS NEEDED FOR ALL PROJECTS

- air-dry clay
- blank note cards and envelopes
- brown paper bags
- cardboard
- colored pencils
- clear acrylic spray or hairspray (optional)
- drinking straws
- fabric paint
- foam board
- glue or decoupage
- iron and ironing board (optional)
- masking tape
- newspaper or cloth to cover your work area
- paint
- paintbrush or foam brush
- paper (plain white and colorful)
- paper plate

- pencil
- picture frame
- ribbon or cord
- rolling pin
- scissors
- sponge
- spoon
- stencils
- straight pins
- string, yarn, or embroidery floss
- T-shirt
- toothpick
- wooden or paper mâché letter
- yarn, string, or embroidery floss

BIRTHDAY GIFTS

Give an extra special birthday gift. Make it yourself! Use string to make **stationery** or an alphabet letter. Decorate a picture frame. Make a nameplate with tiny **sculptures**. Cover a letter **statue** with paper or glitter. Stencil a shirt with fabric paint.

TIP!

When you create the birthday gift yourself, no one else will have a gift like it!

Make note cards for a gift.

Create your own **design**. Or make a name stamp.

Here's How:

1. Cut the cardboard into rectangles or squares.

2. Cover one side of the cardboard with glue.

3. Make a string design in the glue. Or form letters with the string. Use one piece of cardboard per design or letter.

TIP!
You can use a toothpick to move the string in the glue.

4. Paint the string. (Do not paint the cardboard.)

9

5. Turn the stamp over. Press it on the note card.
6. Rub a spoon on the back of the cardboard.
7. Remove the stamp.

Use over and over again!

You can use a string stamp over and over again! Just add more paint to the string and press it again. You can make another print on the same note card. Or you can start a new card. You can also change the color each time you make a print.

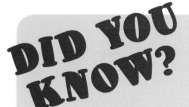

DID YOU KNOW? Making a print with the raised surface of a stamp is called relief printing.

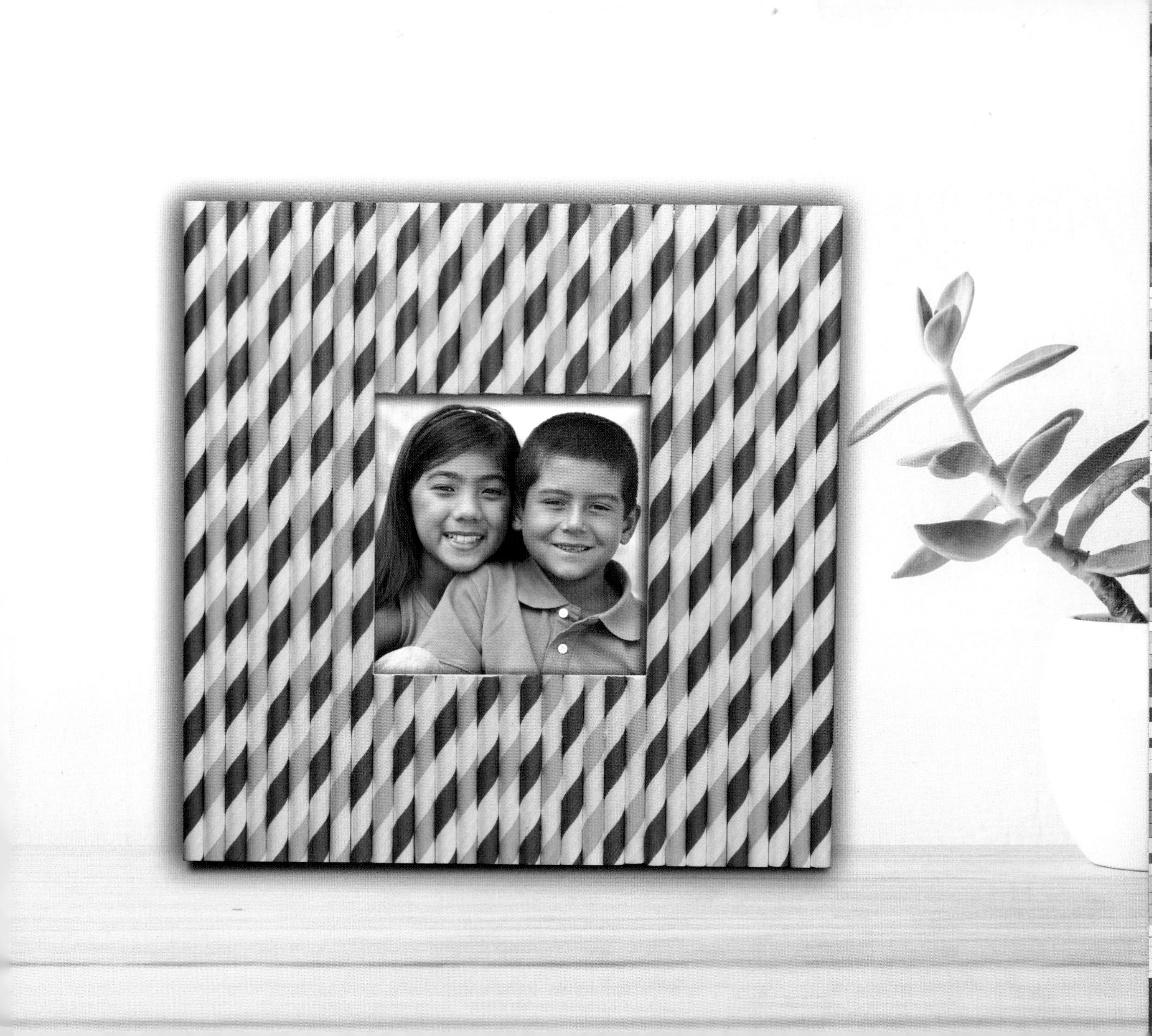

You Will Need:

- small wooden picture frame
- colorful drinking straws
- scissors
- glue
- paintbrush or foam brush (optional)

Cut drinking straws to make a colorful picture frame.

Here's How:

1. Cut the drinking straws to fit the frame.
2. Make a colorful pattern.
4. Cover the frame with glue and straws.
5. Let the glue dry overnight.
6. Place a photo inside the frame.

TIP!
If you don't have a photo, write a "Happy Birthday" note to place inside the frame.

Make your own straws.

You can make your own straws from magazine pages.

Here's How:

1. After you cut out the magazine page, roll it up tightly.
2. Add glue to the edge of the straw before the very last turn.
3. Hold it tight as you count to ten.
4. Let all of the straws dry overnight.

The next day, cut the straws as needed to fit the frame.

TIP!
The page is easier to roll if you start from a corner and roll diagonally.

Make a monogram as your gift. Decorate a letter statue.

Here's How:

1. Cut or tear the paper into small pieces.

DID YOU KNOW?

*A **monogram** is the decorated first initial of someone's name.*

2. Brush a dab of glue on the large letter.

3. Place a piece of paper on the glue.

4. Gently smooth out the paper with your finger. This will remove any air bubbles.

5. Brush over the entire letter with glue and paper.

6. Then seal the letter. Brush glue over the paper. Let the glue dry overnight.

TIP!

Only spread as much glue as you need for the next piece of paper.

Glitter Letters

You can also make monogram letters that sparkle!

Here's How:

1. Cover the letter with glue and shake glitter over it.
2. Use your finger to spread the glitter evenly.
3. Add more glitter and glue as needed.
4. Let the glue dry overnight.

Ask an adult to seal the glitter with hairspray or clear acrylic spray.

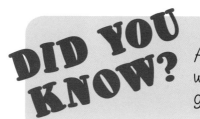

DID YOU KNOW? A standing letter is three-dimensional. It has width, height, and depth for you to cover with glitter or colorful paper.

Make a hanging nameplate.

Here's How:

1. Plan your design with colored pencils and paper.
2. Draw a rectangle.
3. Write the person's name in the middle.
4. Think about any tiny sculptures you can add to make it special.

5. Warm up the clay with your hands.
6. Make a large clay rectangle for the base.
7. Roll the clay into logs so you can make the letters.

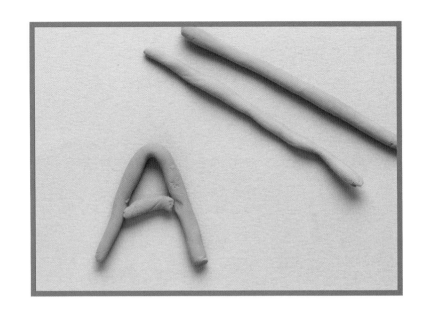

TIP!

Use a rolling pin to make the rectangle flat.

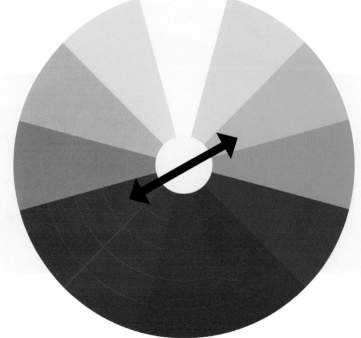

Choose the person's favorite colors. Then add **complementary** colors, the colors on the opposite side of the color wheel.

8. After you form each letter, add it to the base.
9. Spell out the name across the entire rectangle.
10. Add your special touches around the name.
11. Press a pencil into the top corners to make a hole.
12. After the clay dries, tie a ribbon or cord through the holes.

You Will Need:
- newspaper or cloth to cover your work area
- stencils
- fabric paint
- paper plate
- sponge or paintbrush
- brown paper bags or cardboard
- masking tape
- iron and ironing board (optional)
- T-shirt

Stencil a T-shirt.

Make a **personalized** T-shirt with letter stencils. Or make a pretty pattern. It's up to you!

Here's How:

1. Place cardboard or brown paper bags inside the T-shirt.
2. Hold the stencils in place with tape.
3. Pour fabric paint onto a paper plate.

TIP!

Cover the area under the T-shirt so you can paint all the way to the edge of the shirt if necessary.

4. Gently paint the open areas of the stencils.
5. After the paint dries, slowly peel off the stencils.
6. Check the fabric paint directions. They will tell you how to wash and dry the shirt.

TIP!

Some fabric paints must be ironed after they dry. Ask an adult to help you place an old cloth over the shirt and iron it.

Doily Stencils

A paper doily makes a fun stencil. Masking tape will cover up the lacy edges, so use tiny drops of glue to stick the doily to the shirt. After the glue dries, carefully sponge paint onto the doily. Press the paint into the holes in the center. The paint that goes into the holes along the edges will make a scalloped edge.

Write with colorful string.

Here's How:

1. Make a paper letter guide. Draw a large letter, or print one from your home computer.
2. Place the paper letter on the foam board.
3. Place pins around the edge of the letter.

You Will Need:
- newspaper or cloth to cover your work area
- white foam board
- straight pins
- paper letter guide
- pencil
- colorful yarn, string, or embroidery floss
- scissors

4. Remove the letter guide.
5. Wrap string around a pin on the board. Tie a knot.
6. Pull the string over to a new pin.
7. Wrap the string around the new pin.
8. Repeat until you fill the center of the letter.
9. Tie a knot around the last pin. Cut off the extra string.

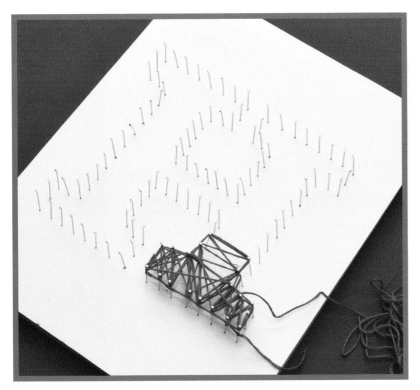

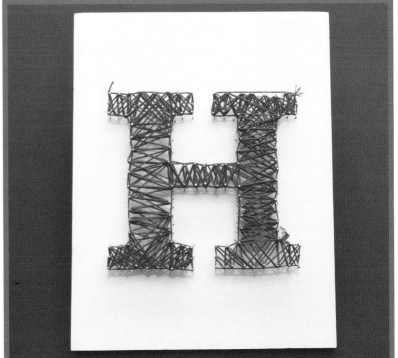

GLOSSARY

complementary (kom-pli-MEN-tuh-ree): in art, opposite colors on the color wheel

design (di-ZINE): to draw something that can be made

monogram (MON-uh-gram): a decorated first initial of someone's name

personalized (PUR-suh-nuhl-ahyzd): something made just for one person

sculptures (SKUHLP-churs): items carved or shaped out of clay

stationery (STAY-shuh-ner-ee): paper and envelopes used to write letters

statue (STACH-oo): a model made from wood, stone, or plastic

INDEX

SHOW WHAT YOU KNOW

1. When making a relief print with a string stamp, why do you only add paint to the string, not the cardboard?

2. How do you change colors when you are making relief prints?

3. Why is it important to smooth out the paper after you glue it down?

4. What makes a statue or a sculpture three-dimensional?

5. Describe how a stencil creates an image when you apply paint.

WEBSITES TO VISIT

http://lifestyle.howstuffworks.com/crafts/paper-crafts/make-stationery.htm

www.diynetwork.com/how-to/make-and-decorate/crafts/how-to-make-a-photo-collage-on-a-big-letter

www.deliacreates.com/sharpie-art-shirts-more-t-shirt/

ABOUT THE AUTHOR

As a child, Anastasia Suen made and wrapped birthday gifts at the kitchen table. Today she uses that same kitchen table to make and wrap birthday gifts in her studio in Northern California.

Meet The Author!
www.meetREMauthors.com

www.rourkeeducationalmedia.com

PHOTO CREDITS: All photos © Blue Door Publishing, FL except the following from Shutterstock.com: pages 4-5 © atsurkan; pages 6 © PhuShutter; page 11 © Wayne0216; photo inside frame, page 11 © Monkey Business images; page 15 background photo without standing monogram © Africa Studio; page 19 background photo without nameplate © Alena Ozerova, photo inside frame © Monkey Business Images; page 20 © Zai Di; page 27 background photo without the letter © rattiya lamrod; page 30 © Mariia Boiko

Edited by: Keli Sipperley

Cover and Interior design by: Nicola Stratford   www.nicolastratford.com
Thank you, Ashley Hayasaka, for making the crafts.

Library of Congress PCN Data

Birthday Gifts / Anastasia Suen
 (Craft It!)
  ISBN 978-1-68342-375-1 (hard cover)
  ISBN 978-1-68342-884-8 (soft cover)
  ISBN 978-1-68342-541-0 (e-Book)
Library of Congress Control Number: 2017931275

Rourke Educational Media
Printed in the United States of America, North Mankato, Minnesota